When I'm Sad...

Moira Butterfield

WAYLAND

First published in 2014 by Wayland
© Wayland 2014

Wayland
Hachette Children's Books
338 Euston Road
London NW1 3BH

Wayland Australia
Level 17/207 Kent Street
Sydney NSW 2000

Produced for Wayland by
White-Thomson Publishing Ltd
www.wtpub.co.uk
+44 (0) 843 208 7460

Editor: Stephen White-Thomson
Design: Rocket Design (East Anglia) Ltd

A catalogue for this title is available from the British Library

ISBN: 9 780 7502 8284 0
e-book ISBN: 9 780 7502 9124 8

Dewey Number: 152.4-dc23

10 9 8 7 6 5 4 3 2 1

Wayland is a division of Hachette Children's Books,
an Hachette UK company.
www.hachette.co.uk

Printed and bound in China

Picture credits:
Shutterstock.com: 3dvin 4, AlenD 5, Mykhaylo Palinchak 6, Belinda
Pretorius 7, Inga Marchuk 8, vectorlib.com 9, Vinicius Tupinamba
10, Warren Goldswain 11, Pressmaster 12, Max Topchii 13, Ilike 14,
Poznyakov 15, Vladimir Melnikov 16, Denis Kuvaev 17, Samuel Borges
Photography 18 - 19, Pressmaster 20, Gelpi JM 21.

I might feel sad if I...

have a bad day...

hurt myself...

break my best toy...

so then I need to get busy!

Take a look and see...

Have you ever had a day...

4

when something happened to make you **feel sad?**

...or your favourite toy **got broken?**

7

Get yourself a **big hug** from someone you love!

Then get as **busy as a bee!**

buzz buzz

busy, busy

Fly a kite!

whoooooosh!

Ride
your bike...

 ...or go for a **swim.**

Bake some yummy cup cakes...

mmmmmmm....

14

...or **paint** a brilliant picture.

15

Do a
funny
dance...

16

...or **sing a song.**

That's a really good one!

Let your head fill with **busy thoughts**.

busy thoughts

18

sad thoughts

They'll
push out
your

sad
thoughts.

19

And soon that sad old day will go away...

...and leave a happy day behind!

Do it!

Can you make a **sad face**?

What sound do you make when **you cry**?

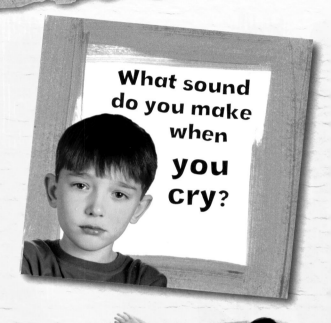

Can you pretend to be as **busy as a bee**?

Can you do a **funny dance**?

Pretend to **fly a kite.**

Pretend to **bake a cake.**

busy thoughts

Imagine your head filling with **busy thoughts.**

Imagine the busy thoughts pushing out all the **sad thoughts.**

sad thoughts

23

Teacher's and parent's notes:

These books are designed for children to explore feelings in a fun interactive way. Encourage them to have fun pointing to the pictures, making sounds and doing some acting, too.

During or after your reading, you could encourage your child to talk further about their own feelings, if they want to. Here are some conversation prompts to try:

Can you remember a time when you felt sad?

Can you think of a good way to stop feeling sad?

Activities to try:

✳ On a piece of paper, draw some sad faces and then some happy faces.

✳ On a piece of paper, draw your favourite picture from this book.

Further reading:

Our Emotions and Behaviour: I'm Not Happy – a book about feeling sad,
written by Sue Graves and illustrated by Desideria Guicciardini (Franklin Watts, 2014)

You Choose! Don't Be Sad, Sam,
written by Lisa Regan and illustrated by Alice Busby (Wayland, 2014)

Your Emotions: I Feel Sad,
written by Brian Moses and illustrated by Mike Gordon (Wayland)